WHAT IN THE WORLD?

FUN-TASTIC PHOTO PUZZLES FOR CURIOUS MINDS

BY JULIE VOSBURGH AGNONE

NATIONAL GEOGRAPHIC

WASHINGTON, D.C.

Look closely among the tangled leaves to see what hangs out in rain forest trees.

HOW TO PLAY

YOUR BRAIN ON PUZZLES! You rely on your vision and your brain to understand the world around you. But as amazing as your eyes are, the pictures they send your brain are quirky: They're upside down, backward, and two-dimensional! Your brain automatically flips the images from your retinas right side up and combines the views from each eye into a three-dimensional image. No wonder picture puzzles can be tough! But puzzles help strengthen your visual perception and cognitive skills, so think of this book as a workout for your brain!

WHAT IN THE WORLD?

Patterns, colors, and shapes help you identify things. The photos in these games show only partial views of animals and objects, which means your brain has to do some heavy lifting to identify what you're seeing. Sound like a challenge that will help bulk up your brain?
HOW TO PLAY: Use photos, written clues, and the scrambled words to find the answers.

SHAPES IN NATURE

Your brain likes to keep things orderly and simple, so it makes sense that the brain wants to automatically group objects according to visual similarities like shape. There are countless shapes in nature, but sometimes we unconsciously interpret random shapes as something we know, seeing letters, hearts, or other shapes in ordinary images. Called interpretation, this brain function helps hone your observation skills and pump up your imagination as you observe objects all around you.
HOW TO PLAY: Recognize the similar shapes, natural and man-made, and identify the objects shown in the photographs.

TAKE A LOOK!

Puzzles like these require you to spend time finding objects, and that helps stretch your attention and memory. While you're searching among a wild jumble of objects for a hockey stick or a treasure chest, you're building brainpower by exercising your concentration skills.
HOW TO PLAY: Find all of the items on the list.

UP CLOSE

Scientists using powerful microscopes can zoom in to reveal stunning details and unseen worlds. The scanning electron microscope

(SEM for short) can magnify objects 500,000 times! You may think you're seeing aliens from another planet, so you'll have to flex your logical thinking muscles to solve these puzzles!

HOW TO PLAY: Match each extreme close-up in the top row with an image in the bottom row.

HIDDEN ANIMALS

Animals often have coloring and patterns that help them blend in with their surroundings and keep them safe from predators. Called camouflage, this trick enables some animals to hide in plain sight! You'll practice attention to detail and visual discrimination strengths with these puzzlers.

HOW TO PLAY: Find the hidden animals in their natural habitats.

OPTICAL ILLUSION

These tricky pics are designed to fool your eyes and brain! Some optical illusions use perspective, an art form that makes flat drawings look 3-D. Because the trick works only from a certain viewpoint, it's all about perception—how your brain interprets conflicting information you're seeing.

HOW TO PLAY: Answer the questions, then take a second look. Is there another way to interpret these wacky photos?

DOUBLE TAKE

Two seemingly similar photographs filled with multicolored objects present a challenge to find a dozen differences between the two images. You will use your visual discrimination—the ability to pick out differences and similarities—as well as exercise concentration and short-term memory.

HOW TO PLAY: Find all of the differences between the two photographs.

MORE CHALLENGES

Ready for the next level? This section offers bonus activities that will expand your brain and build your mental fitness, which boosts your ability to think and learn. It's like having a personal trainer for your brain! Fun activities will extend your cognitive brain skills by relating the puzzling pictures in this book to the real world. Create your own cool optical illusions, test your short- and long-term memory, and see how fast your brain can process exciting new challenges!

Everyone's brain works differently, so don't worry if some of the puzzles are difficult at first. They get easier with practice! Answers on pages 44-46.

This quick-change artist can switch color in 20 seconds!

EMCLAHNEO

FILHNISO

No lyin', there's something fishy about this venomous sea creature.

Go slow and steady like this animal, and you "shell" get the answer.

OOTSRTIE

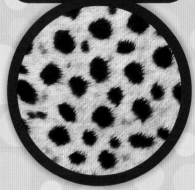

EHAHETC

Running up to 60 miles an hour (97 kph), this is one fast cat.

Yipes!
It's a horse of a different stripe.

AERBZ

This dotty dog is born spotless.

MLATDINAA

AKSEN

Here's the skinny: This reptile often slips away—from its skin.

It's all for love with this fancy feathered show-off.

OACPKCE

IAGFERF

This tall mammal would call Africa its neck of the woods.

ANIMAL PATTERNS # WHAT IN THE WORLD?

SHAPES IN NATURE SPIRALS

The spiral is one of the most beautiful shapes found in nature. A spiral growth pattern often occurs naturally in the mathematically perfect curves of plants, animals, and even formations in space! Can you identify the spirals in the photos shown above? Which one does not naturally grow in a spiral shape?

With your finger, trace the spiral shapes of these snail shells. What do they all have in common?

Fun Fact!

Nature has inspired many **man-made spirals** in art and architecture— even **artificial** islands.

Soccer balls were originally made from **pig bladders.**

< FIND THESE ITEMS ON THE **SPORTS FIELD.** >

4 hockey sticks

3 gloves

3 knee pads

4 helmets

1 hockey puck

9 bowling pins

1 pair of swim goggles

2 tennis balls

4 ice skates

1

2

3

CRIMSON CLOVER

SNOUT BEETLE

MAGGOT

The top row of photographs shows extreme close-ups of the same things that appear in the second row, but in a different order. Match the magnified images with the named objects.

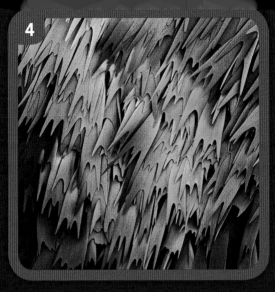

4

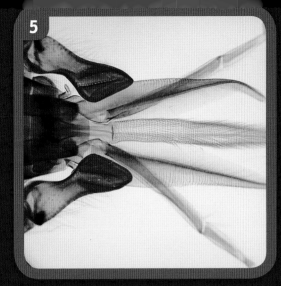

5

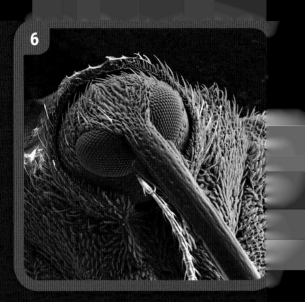

6

JUMPING SPIDER

LUNA MOTH

HONEYBEE

MAGNIFICATION **UP** CLOSE

ORCHID MANTIS

RED IRISH LORD SCULPIN FISH

AFRICAN SCOPS OWL

WALKING LEAF

CRABS   RABBITS

HIDDEN ANIMALS CAMOUFLAGE

Could someone really fall into this crazy volcanic crater? It's actually just a big painting! An artist used perspective, shading, and other tricks to give the flat street some depth. Find out how this amazing optical illusion works on page 44.

Fun Fact!

About **75 percent** of all **volcanoes** are **underwater.**

Fun Fact! **Saturn** is made partly of **helium**—the same gas used to fill **party balloons.**

A crowd of people and balloons jam a street in Sicily, Italy.

FIND 12 DIFFERENCES BETWEEN THESE PHOTOGRAPHS. DOUBLE TAKE

At feeding time,
these swimmers
are never coy.

OKI HISF

TERGI YLLI

Its name is part feline, but it's all flower.

SLABTAKBEL

Dribble, defend, and dunk. Got the point?

This insect is no ruler, but it has the power to go the distance.

ARMONHC
YEUTFTBRL

A fresh and fruity slice means this can't stay round for long.

UTNEPACLOA

MPIKPUN

These tend to get ghoulish grins and make funny faces every fall.

RTEGI

Its striped pattern is as unique as a human's fingerprint.

This orange ape lives the high life— in treetops.

GNNAUTOAR

Crunch a bunch of these for a healthy snack.

RATSCOR

COLOR **WHAT IN THE WORLD?**

TAKE A LOOK!

RAIN FOREST

Fun Fact!

Rainbow-colored **grasshoppers** live in Peru's **rain forests.**

< FIND THESE RAIN FOREST ITEMS. >

1 sloth

3 butterflies

1 tarantula

4 snakes

9 frogs

1 gorilla

3 birds

1 pair of binoculars

1 giant fly

What's the first thing you think of when you see these images? Most people would say "hearts." But it may surprise you to learn that, if seen from a different angle, these things would have nothing in common. Can you name the objects that form these heart shapes?

Heart Reef—a naturally heart-shaped coral formation in Australia's Great Barrier Reef—inspires many marriage proposals when people fly over it.

1

2

3

SILKWORM

HEAD LOUSE

MACAW

Here are more mind-boggling magnifications to mix up your brain!
Match the extreme close-up images on the top row with the named animals.

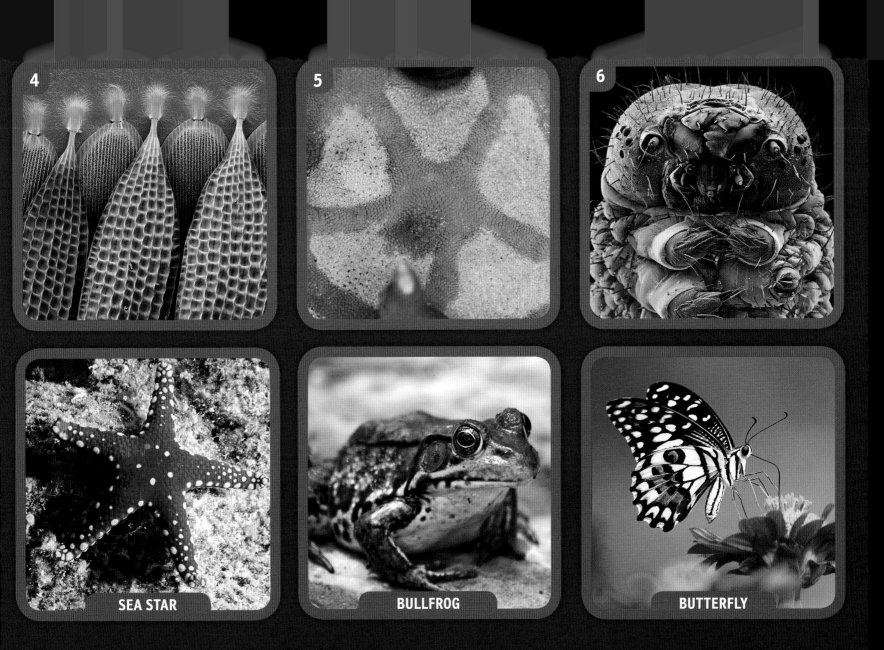

4

5

6

SEA STAR

BULLFROG

BUTTERFLY

MAGNIFICATION **UP** CLOSE

BLACK RHINOCEROS

GRAY TREE FROG

BRITTLE STAR

EURASIAN BITTERN

DWARF CHAMELEON

FROGFISH

HIDDEN ANIMALS CAMOUFLAGE

Fun Fact! Some sharks can swim the length of a soccer field in five seconds.

Is the swimmer floating in the ocean? If you said "yes," the optical illusion of an infinity pool fooled you! This type of swimming pool has a disappearing edge designed to create the visual effect of the water extending into the ocean. See page 45 to find out how this amazing optical illusion works.

< FIND ALL OF THE PIRATE BOOTY. >

6 treasure chests

2 swords

3 cannons

3 eye patches

1 stack of gold bars

1 antique treasure map

1 spyglass

2 hooks

4 bombs

Fun Fact! Cotton candy—the sweet treat we enjoy at carnivals and fairs—was originally called **fairy floss.**

Carnival-goers compete for prizes at the water gun kiosk.

FIND 13 DIFFERENCES BETWEEN THESE PHOTOGRAPHS. **DOUBLE**TAKE

This silent slitherer is one of the forest's most deadly.

RPVEI

SOPREGRASHP

This jumper can't sit still.

HAIRAPN

You wouldn't want to go into a school of these.

Hop out of the way if you see this coming!

Who says cats hate water? This one loves to swim.

OPONIS DRAT GROF

RAGJUA

PITAR

Its long snout tends to taper—to a point.

THOSL

No matter how many toes, they're always slow.

This soaring mammal is totally batty.

If you don't know the answer, wing it.

FINGLY OFX

TCUONA

RAIN FOREST ANIMALS **WHAT** IN THE WORLD?

SHAPES IN NATURE THE ALPHABET

What letters do you see in these objects? There goes your brain again—trying to identify things according to random visual cues! Name these objects in nature that seem to form letters of the alphabet.

Do the three horizontal palm leaves remind you of a capital letter?

CRAB SPIDER

LEAF-TAILED GECKO

ALLIGATOR

WEDDELL SEAL

GAZELLE   ARCTIC HARE

HIDDEN ANIMALS CAMOUFLAGE

Seeing but not believing? That's because your eyes are delivering an image that your brain knows is impossible. This funny photo uses a photography technique called forced perspective. Find out more on page 46.

Fun Fact! Trick photography fools people in many Internet hoaxes.

< FIND THESE ITEMS IN SPACE. >

1 sun

4 astronauts

1 Saturn

1 flag

2 blue planets

1 space shuttle

2 lunar rovers

1 space landing vehicle

4 telescopes

MORE CHALLENGES

IF YOU'RE READY TO TAKE YOUR BRAIN to a whole new level, you're in the right place! These challenging activities will build on the brain skills you've already been developing by relating the puzzling pictures in this book to the world around you.

WHAT IN THE REAL WORLD?

Patterns, colors, and shapes provide fundamental information that triggers your brain to recognize things that you may know. Try these activities to stretch the thinking muscles you started flexing in the "What in the World?" puzzles.

Animal Patterns: pages 6-7
- Start to notice animal patterns all around you—in clothing, rugs, even on wallpaper!
- Use your imagination to think of creative ways an animal pattern could be used in man-made items.

Color: pages 18-19
- All of the objects shown are different shades of orange. How many other orange things can you name?
- Try the same game with other colors.

Rain Forest Animals: pages 32-33
- We instantly recognize a snake by its long, curved shape. Name other animals that have body shapes that are key to identifying them.
- How does the combination of pattern, color, and body shape make certain animals unique?

SEEING SHAPES IN NATURE

There are different shapes everywhere you look in nature. Get outside and try some of these ideas to challenge your observation skills and kick-start your imagination:

- Examine the leaves on trees, bushes, and flowers. Make a list of the different shapes you discover.
- Look at the shapes of insect bodies and animal body parts. What do they remind you of?
- For an active game, set a time limit and compete with friends to see who finds the most shapes on a nature walk.
- Pick out objects that form letters of the alphabet. Can you find letters in nature that spell your name?
- Look up in the sky to see if the clouds have formed interesting shapes. Let your imagination soar!
- What can you see in rock formations or distant mountains?
- Take photographs or make drawings of your observations. What's the most unusual shape you have seen?
- Start a scrapbook to keep track of your shape discoveries and add to it every time you return from exploring.

TAKE ANOTHER LOOK!

There's much more to discover in these puzzles! Here's a list of some ways to test your knowledge:

Sports: pages 10-11

- Count all of the red objects.
- Name at least six sports that use the gear shown in the photograph.
- Which sports items begin with the letter "s"?
- Find all of the objects that involve players using their feet.
- The trophy is for what sport?
- Identify all of the gear used for safety.

Rain Forest: pages 20-21

- Identify all of the reptiles.
- Do you see a rhinoceros beetle?
- Find two baby alligators hatching from eggs.
- Which animals are primates?

Pirate Treasure: pages 28-29

- What country is shown on most of the treasure maps?
- Count the blue jewels.
- Find pictures of the skull and crossbones.
- Identify six undersea creatures. Hint: Coral is an animal!
- Find all of the miniature pirate figures. Which one has a peg leg?
- Count your loot: How many gold coins are there?

Space: pages 38-39

- What planet do you think the striped orange ball represents?
- Count the stars.
- Find one communications satellite.
- Which objects are rockets? Hint: They do not all look the same.

UP CLOSE AND PERSONAL

You may be surprised by what you see when you use a magnifying glass to look at tree bark, a butterfly's wing, your sweater, or anything else that interests you! Here are some fun ways you can get an up close and personal view of everyday items:

- Grab a magnifying glass to become a close-up detective. How close can you get and what do you see?
- If you have access to a microscope, you're in for a treat! Put everyday objects under your microscope and check them out. Some ideas to get you started: a human hair, your pet's hair, a flower leaf, a dead bug, pond water. How do the views differ from what you can see with your naked eye?
- Make drawings of the magnified images you see and ask friends if they can identify what they're seeing.
- Search online for more scanning electron microscope (SEM) photographs that will reveal amazing details of animals, plants, and objects.

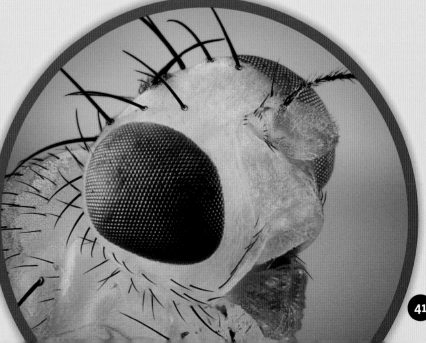

MORE CHALLENGES

SPOTTING HIDDEN ANIMALS

There are hidden animals all around you, whether you live in a city or the country. Often you don't notice them because you're in a hurry or distracted, and they stay hidden because they're afraid. But you may see things if you look around and stay quiet when you're outside. Here's how to improve your observation and visual discrimination skills while watching animals in their natural habitats. Caution: Be sure to keep your distance from wild animals!

- Sit quiet and motionless and just observe. You can do this anywhere—in your backyard, a park, forest, desert, or beach.
- After five minutes, write down some details you didn't notice before you stopped.
- How many different plants and animals are there around you? Look carefully to spot even the smallest insects!
- Snap a photo! Try photographing the animal from various angles to get the best light and perspective.

CREATING OPTICAL ILLUSIONS

Have you ever wanted to stand on top of a bottle like the person appears to do in the photo on page 37? You can create your own optical illusions using the forced perspective technique and your camera. Think about the image you'd like to create. For example, you could show someone balancing a miniature version of your best friend in their hand. Here's how:

- Line up one friend in the background and another in the foreground. Have the foreground friend hold out their hand with the palm up. The background friend can stand on one leg or act silly.
- Play around with the distance between the two and between you and the foreground friend. The background friend needs to be far enough away to appear small.
- Carefully line up the shot and snap the picture.
- Play around with your camera's focus settings. If you have autofocus, try to focus on something between the two subjects. If you have a manual-focus camera, use a large f-stop and try to get both subjects in focus.

DOUBLE TAKE TWO

Want to quiz your friends and fool your family with more puzzles like the "Double Take" games in this book? Try these activities as a group:

- For a short-term memory workout, go back to the photographs on pages 16-17. Spend a few minutes finding the differences between the two images. Then close the book and write down as many of the differences as you can remember. Repeat the exercise using pages 30-31.

- For a long-term memory test, do the same exercise as above, but look at the photographs in the morning and wait until evening—or the next day—to write the list.

- Now use the pictures to see how observant you are. Study one of the pictures for a few minutes, then close the book. Describe specific details of the photograph to a friend. How did you do?

- Take a picture of an ordinary scene such as your room, your backyard, or a park. Change ten things and reshoot the photograph. Print the two pictures and make a game out of finding their differences.

- Practice doing picture puzzles with a timer to increase your brain's processing speed.

SHHH! ANSWERS

Fun Fact!

Your brain **generates** enough electricity to power a **lightbulb.**

TITLE PAGE
(pages 2-3)

An oriental whip snake uses camouflage to hide in the rain forest.

WHAT IN THE WORLD?
(pages 6-7)

Top row: chameleon, tortoise, lionfish, zebra, cheetah. **Bottom row:** Dalmatian, snake, peacock, giraffe.

SHAPES IN NATURE
(pages 8-9)

Top row: fern, hedge maze, galaxy. **Bottom row:** ammonite fossil, cabbage, chameleon tail. A hedge does not grow in a spiral shape naturally.

TAKE A LOOK!
(pages 10-11)

UP CLOSE
(pages 12-13)

1. maggot, 2. crimson clover, 3. jumping spider, 4. luna moth, 5. honeybee, 6. snout beetle.

HIDDEN ANIMALS
(page 14)

OPTICAL ILLUSION
(page 15)

Illusion explained: Sidewalk artist Edgar Mueller painted this scene on a street in Germany. It has so much detail that it looks three-dimensional when viewed from a certain angle, or perspective. This technique is called anamorphic art. It may have been inspired by a 17th-century 3-D painting technique that was used to make flat church ceilings appear to have a dome effect.

DOUBLE TAKE
(pages 16-17)

WHAT IN THE WORLD?
(pages 18-19)

Top row: koi fish, monarch butterfly, tiger lily, cantaloupe, basketball. **Bottom row:** orangutan, pumpkin, carrots, tiger.

TAKE A LOOK!
(pages 20-21)

SHAPES IN NATURE
(pages 22-23)

Top row: clouds, stone-enclosed pool, penguin chick. **Bottom row:** cross section of a tree, flamingos, prickly pear cactus.

UP CLOSE
(pages 24-25)

1. macaw, 2. bullfrog, 3. head louse, 4. butterfly, 5. sea star, 6. silkworm.

HIDDEN ANIMALS
(page 26)

OPTICAL ILLUSION
(page 27)

Illusion explained: The water in an infinity pool reaches the top of the pool and spills invisibly over the edge. Your eyes are imagining a three-dimensional scene, and the illusion takes advantage of your understanding of the physical world. Because you can't see the expected edge of the pool, you are fooled into thinking that the pool water extends into the deeper, darker water of the ocean in the distance.

TAKE A LOOK!
(pages 28-29)

DOUBLE TAKE
(pages 30-31)

WHAT IN THE WORLD?
(pages 32-33)

Top row: viper, poison dart frog, grasshopper, jaguar, piranha. **Bottom row:** flying fox, tapir, toucan, sloth.

SHHH! ANSWERS

SHAPES IN NATURE
(pages 34-35)

Top row: moss-covered cedar tree—A, tree branch—K, caterpillar—L. **Bottom row:** rock formation—O, fern—P, spider in web—X.

HIDDEN ANIMALS
(page 36)

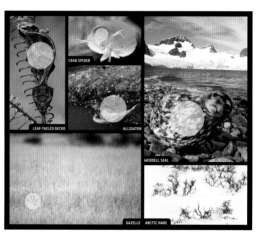

OPTICAL ILLUSION
(page 37)

Illusion explained: Photographers often create optical illusions like this one using the forced perspective technique. This photo foolery makes a large object in the background seem smaller, while a small object placed close to the camera appears larger. The unexpected perspective forces the viewer into misinterpreting the image. Funny trick!

TAKE A LOOK!
(pages 38-39)

Fun Fact! Your eyes process more than **120 million** bits of information every second.

MORE TO EXPLORE

HAVE FUN EXPLORING more optical illusions, puzzles, and games with these websites, books, and other resources.

WEBSITES

kids.nationalgeographic.com
This site inspires curious kids and makes learning fun. Check out the games section!

kids.niehs.nih.gov/index.htm
Discover tons of games at this site from the National Institute of Environmental Health Sciences.

kidskonnect.com
A safe Internet gateway that is loaded with brain games just for kids.

lumosity.com
A website where people of all ages can build a personalized brain-training program.

BOOKS & MAGAZINES

Xtreme Illusions
National Geographic, 2012
A mind-bending collection of visual puzzles that will amaze your friends, mystify your family, and blow your own mind!

The Big Book of Fun!
National Geographic, 2010
Check out these boredom-busting games, jokes, puzzles, mazes, and more!

Complete Guide to Brain Health
By Michael S. Sweeney
National Geographic, 2013
A book for the whole family to learn simple exercises that can strengthen your brain.

Brain Works
By Michael S. Sweeney
National Geographic, 2011
This book for adults and kids reveals the mind-bending science of how you see, what you think, and who you are. Includes cool optical illusions.

National Geographic Kids magazine
Dare to explore! Look for visual games and activities in the "Fun Stuff" department.

TELEVISION

Grab a parent and tune in to **Brain Games** on the National Geographic Channel.
Parents: **braingames.nationalgeographic.com**

CREDITS

PUBLISHED BY THE NATIONAL GEOGRAPHIC SOCIETY

John M. Fahey, *Chairman of the Board and Chief Executive Officer*

Declan Moore, *Executive Vice President; President, Publishing and Travel*

Melina Gerosa Bellows, *Executive Vice President; Chief Creative Officer, Books, Kids, and Family*

PREPARED BY THE BOOK DIVISION

Hector Sierra, *Senior Vice President and General Manager*

Nancy Laties Feresten, *Senior Vice President, Kids Publishing and Media*

Jennifer Emmett, *Vice President, Editorial Director, Children's Books*

Eva Absher-Schantz, *Design Director, Kids Publishing and Media*

Jay Sumner, *Director of Photography, Children's Publishing*

R. Gary Colbert, *Production Director*

Jennifer A. Thornton, *Director of Managing Editorial*

STAFF FOR THIS BOOK

Kate Olesin, *Project Editor*

James Hiscott, Jr., *Art Director/Designer*

Lisa Jewell, *Senior Photo Editor*

Ariane Szu-Tu, *Editorial Assistant*

Callie Broaddus, *Design Production Assistant*

Hillary Moloney, *Associate Photo Editor*

Julie Vosburgh Agnone, *Writer*

Grace Hill, *Associate Managing Editor*

Joan Gossett, *Production Editor*

Lewis R. Bassford, *Production Manager*

Susan Borke, *Legal and Business Affairs*

PRODUCTION SERVICES

Phillip L. Schlosser, *Senior Vice President*

Chris Brown, *Vice President, NG Book Manufacturing*

George Bounelis, *Vice President, Production Services*

Nicole Elliott, *Manager*

Rachel Faulise, *Manager*

Robert L. Barr, *Manager*

The National Geographic Society is one of the world's largest nonprofit scientific and educational organizations. Founded in 1888 to "increase and diffuse geographic knowledge," the Society's mission is to inspire people to care about the planet. It reaches more than 400 million people worldwide each month through its official journal, *National Geographic*, and other magazines; National Geographic Channel; television documentaries; music; radio; films; books; DVDs; maps; exhibitions; live events; school publishing programs; interactive media; and merchandise. National Geographic has funded more than 10,000 scientific research, conservation, and exploration projects and supports an education program promoting geographic literacy.

FOR MORE INFORMATION, please visit www.nationalgeographic.com, call 1-800-NGS LINE (647-5463), or write to the following address:

National Geographic Society
1145 17th Street N.W.
Washington, D.C. 20036-4688 U.S.A.

Visit us online at www.nationalgeographic.com/books

For librarians and teachers: www.ngchildrensbooks.org

More for kids from National Geographic:
kids.nationalgeographic.com

For information about special discounts for bulk purchases, please contact National Geographic Books Special Sales:
ngspecsales@ngs.org

For rights or permissions inquiries, please contact National Geographic Books Subsidiary Rights: ngbookrights@ngs.org

Trade edition ISBN: 978-1-4263-1517-6
Library edition ISBN: 978-1-4263-1608-1

Printed in China

13/RRDS/1